Desert Animals

Biome Beasts

D0339804

Lisa Colozza Cocca

Rourke
Educational Media
rourkeeducationalmedia.com

A Division of
Carson Dellosa Education

BEFORE AND DURING READING ACTIVITIES

Before Reading: *Building Background Knowledge and Vocabulary*

Building background knowledge can help children process new information and build upon what they already know. Before reading a book, it is important to tap into what children already know about the topic. This will help them develop their vocabulary and increase their reading comprehension.

Questions and Activities to Build Background Knowledge:

1. Look at the front cover of the book and read the title. What do you think this book will be about?
2. What do you already know about this topic?
3. Take a book walk and skim the pages. Look at the table of contents, photographs, captions, and bold words. Did these text features give you any information or predictions about what you will read in this book?

Vocabulary: *Vocabulary Is Key to Reading Comprehension*

Use the following directions to prompt a conversation about each word.

- Read the vocabulary words.
- What comes to mind when you see each word?
- What do you think each word means?

> **Vocabulary Words:**
> - *adaptation*
> - *burrows*
> - *dew*
> - *dunes*
> - *glands*
> - *nocturnal*
> - *precipitation*
> - *predators*
> - *prey*
> - *sensitivity*

During Reading: *Reading for Meaning and Understanding*

To achieve deep comprehension of a book, children are encouraged to use close reading strategies. During reading, it is important to have children stop and make connections. These connections result in deeper analysis and understanding of a book.

Close Reading a Text

During reading, have children stop and talk about the following:

- Any confusing parts
- Any unknown words
- Text to text, text to self, text to world connections
- The main idea in each chapter or heading

Encourage children to use context clues to determine the meaning of any unknown words. These strategies will help children learn to analyze the text more thoroughly as they read.

When you are finished reading this book, turn to the next-to-last page for **Text-Dependent Questions** and an **Extension Activity**.

Table of Contents

Biomes

A biome is a large region of Earth with living things that have adapted to the conditions of that region.

NORTH AMERICA

SOUTH
AMERICA

 = Hot Desert

 = Semiarid Desert

= Cold Desert

Desert biomes receive less than 20 inches (51 centimeters) of **precipitation** each year. There are hot deserts, semiarid deserts, and cold deserts. Deserts near oceans are coastal deserts.

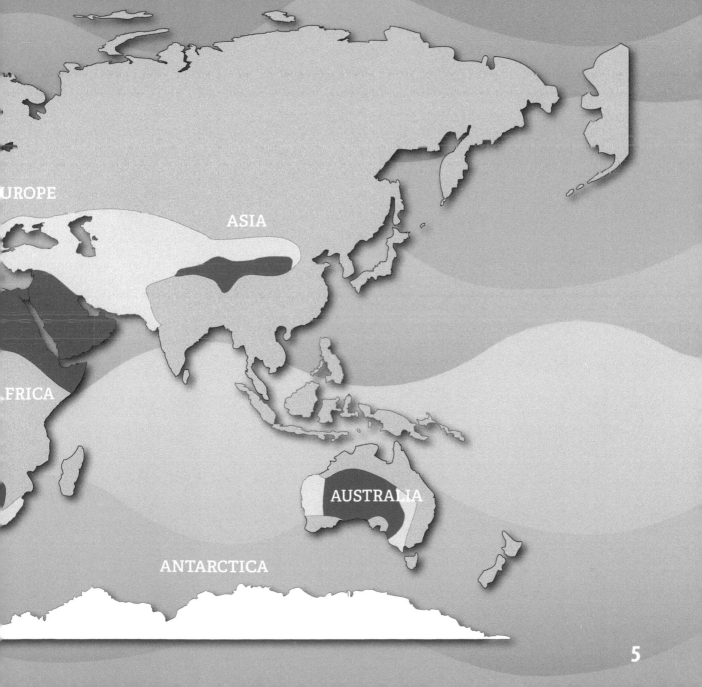

Hot Deserts

There are hot deserts in North Africa, the southwestern United States, Mexico, and Australia. Fall, winter, and spring are warm. Summer is hot. Temperatures sometimes reach 114 degrees Fahrenheit (46 degrees Celsius).

These deserts usually receive less than 12 inches (30.5 centimeters) of rain each year. Ground-hugging shrubs, woody trees, and cactus grow here.

Did You Know?

The thorny devil lives in the hot desert. It has grooves between its scales, which collect **dew** drops at night. The water runs through the grooves and into the lizard's mouth.

The horned viper is one of the many snakes living in hot deserts. Some scientists think the scales over its eyes might be an **adaptation** to protect the eyes from the sand.

The horned viper is a sidewinder. It moves by throwing loops of its body ahead. Only two points of its body are in contact with the hot sand at one time.

Most mammals here are **nocturnal**, including the fennec fox. It is the smallest kind of fox. Its big ears release heat from its body. Its long, thick golden hair covers even the soles of its feet. The hair keeps the fox warm at night and protects its feet from hot sand.

Did You Know?

The kangaroo rat lives in the hot desert. It gets water from the seeds it eats. It has no sweat **glands**, so water loss is low.

Several kinds of birds, such as greater roadrunners, have adapted to the hot desert. Greater roadrunners can fly, but they are better at running. They get water from the foods they eat, such as bugs, lizards, and rodents. Their bodies reabsorb water, rather than expel it. Special nasal glands remove extra salt and slow water loss.

Semiarid Deserts

Semiarid deserts have long, dry, warm-to-hot summers. These deserts usually receive more precipitation than hot deserts. Low bushes, brush, and sage grow here.

Did You Know?

The sky above the semiarid desert can be busy. Birds, from tiny hummingbirds to large vultures, live here. Insects, such as bees and flies, are also a part of this biome.

Did You Know?

The desert tortoise is active only during rainy times. It has an extra-large bladder that can store 40 percent of the tortoise's body weight in water.

The chuckwalla, like all reptiles, is cold-blooded. Its body temperature changes with the temperature of the air around it. The desert gets cold at night. The chuckwalla moves very slowly when it is cold. **Predators** can easily catch it, so the lizard hides between rocks at night. In the day, it stays in the hot sun until its body warms.

Many mammals here, such as the skunk, avoid the hot day by staying in underground **burrows**. Others, like the jackrabbit, remain above ground. Jackrabbits have fur on the soles of their feet for protection from hot sand. They rest under bushes during the hottest hours of the day.

Did You Know?

If the air temperature reaches 104 degrees Fahrenheit (40 degrees Celsius), the blood flow slows in the jackrabbit's ears. The ears then lay back onto the head. This keeps the jackrabbit from overheating.

Many scorpions and spiders live in this biome too. The two-toned wolf spider blends in with the sand it burrows into during the day. Excellent night vision helps it hunt in the dark. Its high **sensitivity** to ground vibrations helps keep the spider from being another animal's dinner.

Coastal Deserts

Coastal deserts have cool winters and warm summers. They average three to five inches (8 to 13 centimeters) of rain each year. Bushes, brush, and rice grasses grow here.

Many snakes live in coastal deserts, including Peringuey's adder. Most snakes have eyes on the sides of their heads, but this adder's eyes are on the top. When the snake buries its body in the sand, it can still see because of its eye location. It can catch a passing lizard for dinner without being seen.

Did You Know?

The coastal deserts are home to more than 60 kinds of lizards.

Many mammals found on savannas have adapted to life in coastal deserts. The elephants in coastal deserts have smaller bodies, longer legs, and broader feet than elephants in savannas. These adaptations help elephants cross the desert and climb over sand **dunes** to reach a watering hole.

Another adaptation is that elephants here travel in small groups instead of in large herds. This way, there are fewer animals sharing the water.

Did You Know?

Elephants remember water hole locations. If the hole is dry, the elephant digs into the sand looking for water. If no water is found, it will walk miles to the next hole.

darkling beetle

Few insects live in this biome. The darkling beetle, however, has adapted to coastal desert conditions. The beetle climbs to the top of a sand dune at dawn and stands on its head. Its wing cases collect droplets of dew rolling in off the ocean. The dew rolls down through the wings and into the beetle's mouth.

Frogs and toads need moisture to reproduce. Some toads in coastal deserts produce a jellylike substance that seals their burrow during the dry spell. They remain inside for eight to nine months until a heavy rainfall. Then, they move to a watering hole where they lay their eggs. The toad's life cycle in the coastal desert is short. It moves through all stages of growth before the water dries up.

desert toad

Owls, eagles, and vultures live in coastal deserts. They get their water from the food they eat.

Humboldt penguins nest in the coastal desert in South America. The penguins drink salt water and eat fish from the ocean. Unlike cold-climate penguins, these birds are not completely covered by feathers. They have pink patches of skin around their eyes and bills that release heat from their bodies.

Cold Deserts

Cold deserts have long, freezing winters and short, cold summers. Precipitation comes as snow. Antarctica is a cold desert. About 98 percent of it is covered by ice. There are no trees, bushes, or cold-blooded animals in this biome.

Arctic wolf

Did You Know?

Like most cold desert mammals, the Arctic wolf has two layers of fur. It also has padded paws to help it move on the frozen ground.

The Arctic fox's warm, thick fur is white in winter and brown in summer. Its short, wide, front-facing ears provide the fox with excellent hearing. The fox can hear **prey** moving below the snow. It jumps into the air and pounces through the snow and onto the prey.

Arctic fox

There are about 46 kinds of birds in Antarctica. They all have waterproof feathers with a second layer of feathers underneath. Most of them spend only part of the year in this biome.

Emperor penguins spend about four months of the year nesting on the cold desert. During this time, they enter the nearby ocean for food and water.

They are the largest kind of penguin. They have plenty of body fat and several layers of feathers. Their size, fat, and feathers help them keep warm. Emperor penguins are also social and will huddle together to stay warm.

Desert biomes can be hot, semiarid, coastal, or cold. They have little precipitation. Many animals have adapted to the extreme conditions found in these biomes.

ACTIVITY:
Does the Adaptation Fit?

Many of the animals in this book have special adaptations that allow them to fit into the biome. What if they were moved to a different biome? Would those old adaptations make the animals a good fit for their new biome or would they need to adapt again?

Supplies

- paper
- pencil
- markers or crayons

Directions

1. Choose an animal from one of the desert biomes in this book.
2. Think about what adaptations help that animal survive in that biome.
3. Choose a different biome such as a grassland, forest, or ocean.
4. Draw a picture of the animal you chose as it might look as part of the new biome. What adaptations would it need to make?
5. Label the new adaptations on your drawing.

Glossary

adaptation (ad-ap-TAY-shuhn): a change a living thing goes through that allows it to better fit into its surroundings

burrows (BUR-ohs): tunnels, holes, or dens dug under the surface of the ground and used as animal homes

dew (doo): small water droplets that form overnight and collect on surfaces outside

dunes (doons): hills formed when wind or water tides drop sand in an area

glands (glands): cells, groups of cells, or organs that produce or release natural body chemicals

nocturnal (nahk-TUR-nuhl): active at night

precipitation (pri-sip-i-TAY-shuhn): water that falls from clouds in the form of rain, snow, sleet, or hail

predators (PRED-uh-turs): animals that hunt other animals for food

prey (pray): an animal that is hunted by another animal for food

sensitivity (sen-si-TIV-i-tee): a sharp awareness of change or movement

Index

Text-Dependent Questions

1. What are the four kinds of desert biomes?

2. Describe how a sidewinder moves.

3. Why is life in semiarid deserts a challenge for reptiles?

4. How are elephants in coastal deserts different from elephants on savannas?

5. Compare and contrast Humboldt and emperor penguins.

Extension Activity

Look for and read several poems about life in the desert. Note the kinds of details they include. Then, write a poem about one or more of the desert biomes based on what you learned from this book. Illustrate the poem.

About the Author

Lisa Colozza Cocca has enjoyed reading and learning new things for as long as she can remember. She lives in New Jersey by the coast and loves the feel of the sand in her toes. You can learn more about Lisa and her work at www.lisacolozzacocca.com.

www.rourkeeducationalmedia.com

PHOTO CREDITS: Cover & Title Pg ©Lisay, ©Schroptschop, ©NNehring, ©Jay Iwasaki; Pg 3, 10, 11, 14, 16, 20, 24, 28, 30, 32 ©Pobytov; Pg 5 ©ttsz, ©CarlaNichiata; Pg 6 ©JanelleLugge, ©tonda; Pg 7 ©Mark Kostich; Pg 8 ©acceptfoto; Pg 9 ©Nicholas Taffs, ©Saddako; Pg 10 ©SweetyMommy; Pg 11 ©Kenneth Canning, ©helovi; Pg 12 ©estivillml, ©abishome; Pg 14 ©SteveByland; Pg 15 ©KevinDyer; Pg 16 ©David Havel, ©Maurizio Lanini; Pg 18 ©JurgaR; Pg 20 ©NaniP; Pg 21 ©Bernhard Richter; Pg 22 ©Png-Studio; Pg 24 ©Tony Campbell, ©LeFion; Pg 26 ©VargaJones; Pg 28 ©marekuliasz;

Edited by: Kim Thompson
Cover and interior design by: Kathy Walsh

Library of Congress PCN Data

Desert Animals / Lisa Colozza Cocca
(Biome Beasts)
ISBN 978-1-73161-441-4 (hard cover)
ISBN 978-1-73161-236-6 (soft cover)
ISBN 978-1-73161-546-6 (e-Book)
ISBN 978-1-73161-651-7 (ePub)
Library of Congress Control Number: 2019932141

Rourke Educational Media

CPSIA information can be obtained
at www.ICGtesting.com
Printed in the USA
BVHW062305090522
636537BV00001B/1